100 Ways to Be in Joy

by Halle Eavelyn

100 Ways to Be in Joy by Halle Eavelyn.

ISBN: 978-1544953168

Visit our website at www.halleeavelyn.com.

This book is for all my clients (past, present and future) so that they — and YOU — can begin to add more joy into their lives.

You will find that even doing a few of these things will make a huge difference.

For Marlen, for showing me the way.

Wear something you love

 1

Smell fresh-cut herbs

 2

Get sand between your toes

 3

Plant a tree

 4

Buy a meal for a homeless person

 5

Attend a cultural or street festival

The path to joy can begin with the smallest of steps.

Eat something you loved as a child

 **7**

Visit a sacred site

 8

Swim with dolphins

 9

Talk with — or listen to — positive people

10

Ride a ferris wheel

11

Everyone needs joy
in their lives.

Rollerblade

Write a song...or a poem...or a story

 **13**

Host a brunch, or a dinner party

14

Write down ten things you're grateful for

15

Listen to a baby laugh

 **16**

Drink Champagne at sunset

17

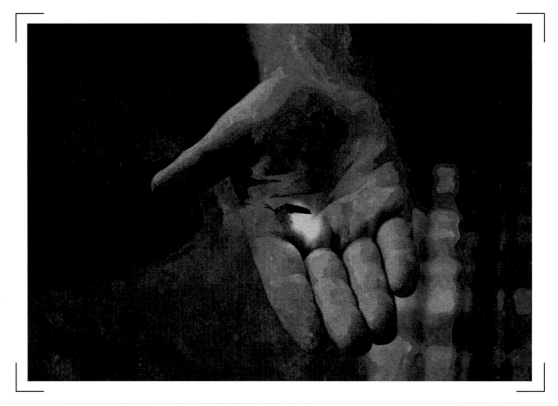

Rescue a bug

18

The more joy you have,
the easier everything
else will seem.

Smell things baking

 **19**

Swing

20

Ride a horse

Lie down in the grass

22

Buy yourself flowers

23

Visit art at a museum or gallery

 **24**

Read aloud to someone who can't

25

Go kayaking

Choose activities, no matter how simple, that bring you joy.

Do something that surprises you

27

Play something uplifting

 **28**

Hug a child

29

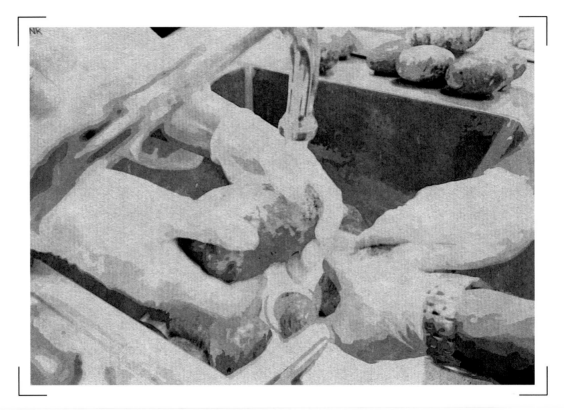

Volunteer in a soup kitchen

30

Ride a carousel

31

No matter what has happened to you in your life, you deserve joy.

Go whitewater rafting...or skydiving...or parasailing

32

See fireworks

33

Stretch – physically, mentally, spiritually

 **34**

Pet a cat

Savor a cup of coffee

 **36**

See live theater — sit close

37

Take a sunset sail

38

God, Spirit, the Universe... whatever you call it, it wants you to feel joy.

Sleep naked in really yummy sheets

39

Dance

40

Ride a bike for fun

41

Visit a new country

 **42**

Pay it forward

 **43**

Go swimming, preferably in a lake or ocean

 **44**

We have been put here on this planet so that God can feel joy uniquely, through each of us.

Volunteer on a community project

45

Take a bubble bath

46

Go to a concert

47

Taste something delicious

 **48**

Learn to salsa

49

Hang little white lights

50

Tell someone you love them — any way you like

51

People always ask me,
"What is my purpose?"
The answer is: You have
come here to be, and
to be in joy.

Curl up with a good book

52

Visit a beautiful place of worship

 **53**

Volunteer at a cause event, like a 5K or a bike ride

 **54**

Play with a dog

55

Observe a butterfly

56

Eat when you are truly hungry

Celebrate as often as possible

Listen to your favorite music

 **59**

Share something important

60

Yes, there will be sorrow and pain. But those things only negate joy if we let them.

Do yoga

61

Be open to the new & unexpected, even if it's uncomfortable

Learn to tap dance

Smell the flowers

64

Smile — at everybody

65

There is so much power in joy — the simple pleasure of being present in each moment of it.

Sing in a choir...or in the shower

Play with a child

Skip

68

Turn your car into a prayer chamber

69

Make someone laugh

 **70**

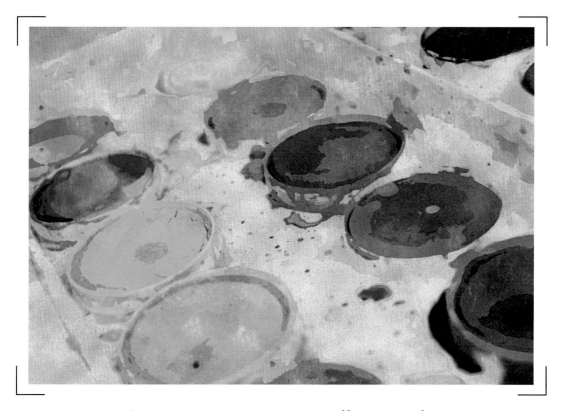

Paint a painting...or a wall...or a chair

71

Watch the tide come in

 **72**

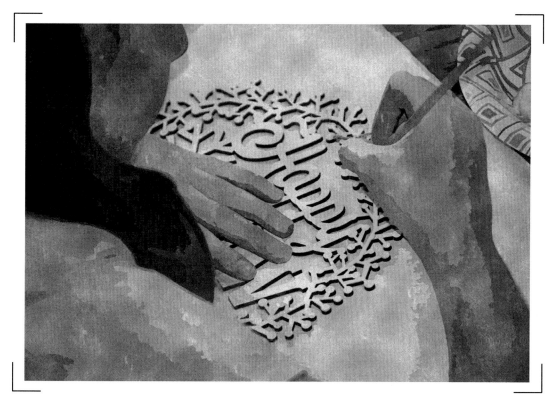

Scrapbook, color, or craft

73

Want more joy in your life?

Keep calling it in.

Set up a birdhouse or feeder and watch what happens

Plant vegetables or herbs

75

Walk or hike in the mountains

76

Garden...or visit a garden

77

Work out

78

Go out on a boat

79

Like attracts like.
Joy attracts joy.

Walk in the woods

80

Pet a pony

81

Be in the present moment...don't think about the future or the past

 **82**

Listen to waves crashing on the shore

 **83**

Make snow angels

 **84** ∽

Listen to live music

 **85**

Try a new cuisine

86

Joy is always there. When you choose to see it, it can work its magic on you.

Meditate (why not try a new way...there are many)

Color

Smell a baby's head

89

Write in your journal

 **90**

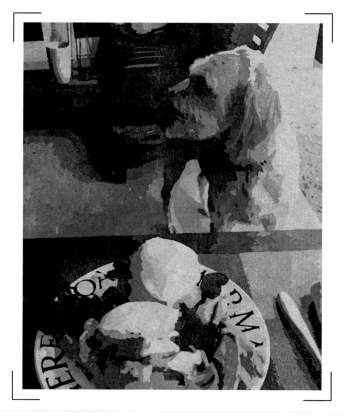

Cook something from scratch

No one ever said,
"I have too much joy
in my life."

Play tennis

92

Relax in a hammock

93

Play an instrument

 94

Beachcomb

95

Eat colorful and healthy

96

Enjoy a rainy afternoon

 **97**

Meet people from other cultures

 **98**

When Joy shows up,
remember to say,
"Yes, please...more...
and thank you!"

See your favorite movie again

 **99**

Seek joy in all things
(whenever possible, remember you always have a choice)

∽ **100** ∼

BONUS: YOUR WAY
Whatever you choose is best for you. Just keep choosing JOY!

 **101**

Photo credits

2. Smell fresh-cut herbs © Alexander Raths | Dreamstime.com

3. Get sand between your toes © Marlen Rodriguez

6. Balinese street festival © Spirit Quest Tours

8. Temple of Seti I at Abydos © Spirit Quest Tours

9. Swim with dolphins ©Leigh Hilbert Photography; SparkyLeigh via Visual Hunt

12. Rollerblade © Martinmark | Dreamstime.com

15. Write down ten things you're grateful for © monkeybusiness via Deposit Photos

18. Rescue a bug © theloushe via Visual hunt

21. Ride a horse © ClaraDon via Visualhunt

22. Lie down in the grass © Marlen Rodriguez

24. Visit a museum or gallery ©Stuck in Customs via VisualHunt.com

25. Read aloud © Godfer | Dreamstime.com

26. Go kayaking © Ingo Osterheld

27. Do something that surprises you © Nicolas Alejandro Street Photography via Visualhunt

30. Volunteer in a soup kitchen © USDAgov via VisualHunt.com

31. Ride a carousel © Marlen Rodriguez

35. Pet a cat © BWCK Photography via VisualHunt

37. See live theater © Luis Torres

39. Sleep naked © tizzie via Visualhunt.com

41. Ride a bike for fun © miroslav0108 via Visualhunt

43. Pay It Forward © Lucian Coman | Dreamstime.com

45. Volunteer on a community project © danielthornton via VisualHunt.com

46. Take a bubble bath © Georgii Dolgykh | Dreamstime.com

Photo credits

49. Learn to salsa ©Dance Photographer - Brendan Lally via VisualHunt

50. Hang little white lights © Wonderlane via VisualHunt.com

52. Curl up with a good book © alexraths via Deposit Photos

53. Ar Rafai Mosque © Spirit Quest Tours

57. Eat when you are truly hungry © Ariwasabi | Dreamstime.com

60. Share something important © bp6316 via VisualHunt.com

63. Learn to tap dance © Steve Snodgrass via Visual Hunt

64. Smell the flowers ©Photoruan via visualhunt.com

65. Smile — at everybody © web4camguy via Visualhunt.com

68. Skip © michelle jaciubek via Visualhunt.com

75. Plant vegetables or herbs © Barbara Helgason | Dreamstime.com

80. Walk in the woods © Michele Cedzich

81. Pet a pony © La Novella Orchidea via VisualHunt

82. Be in the Present Moment - © Jonathan Kos-Read via VisualHunt.com

83. Listen to waves crashing on the shore ©Wendy Vitalich, from her book, Ocean Blessings,

to order: woceanblessings@gmail.com

92. Play tennis © Steven Pisano via Visualhunt.com

99. See your favorite movie again © Monkeybusinessimages | Dreamstime.com

Thanks

Melissa Etheridge and Sheryl Crow
for their concert to support the
Dolphins Cancer Challenge

Pixabay
for its awesome catalog of free images

VisualHunt
for its great catalog of free images

Dreamstime & DepositPhotos
for their royalty-free images

Sketcher
for its remarkable app!

Michele Cedzich & Wendy Vitalich
for their lovely photos

Made in the USA
Lexington, KY
05 February 2018